Modern World Religions

Judaism

Cavan Wood

D1324016

00 741077 01

To Sarah for her love and support

Heinemann Educational Publishers
Halley Court, Jordan Hill, Oxford, OX2 8EJ
Part of Harcourt Education

Heinemann is the registered trademark of
Harcourt Education Limited

Text © Cavan Wood, 2002

First published in 2002

06 05 04
10 9 8 7 6 5 4 3

British Library Cataloguing in Publication Data
A catalogue record for this book is available from the
British Library

ISBN 0 435 33643 6

Typeset by Artistix, Thame, Oxon
Printed and bound in Spain by Edelvives

Acknowledgements
The publishers would like to thank the London Beth Din,
Kashrut Division, for permission to use the kosher
certificate, p. 19.

The publishers would like to thank the following for
permission to use photographs: Andes Press Agency/
Carlos Reyes-Manzo, pp. 14, 16 (bottom right), 23 (top),
24 (top), 43; BFI Stills, p. 2 (left); The Bridgeman Art Library/
Galleria degli Uffizi, Florence, p. 5; The Bridgeman Art
Library/Magyar Nemzeti Galeria, Budapest, p. 58; The
Bridgeman Art Library/The Mass Gallery, London, p. 12;
The Bridgeman Art Library/Museum of the City of New
York, p. 49; Camera Press/Titti Fabi, p. 3 (right); Camera
Press/Amram Galmi/Imapress, p .13; Camera Press/Lee
Lynx, p. 6; Camera Press/Greg Marinovich, p. 28; Camera
Press/Richard Stonehouse, pp. 3 (left), 8; Camera
Press/Kevin Unger, p. 48; Corbis, p. 56; Mary Evans
Picture Library, p. 55; Impact/John Evans, p. 52; Alex
Keene, p. 17; Performing Arts Library/Mark Douet, p. 2
(right); Zev Radovan, pp. 10, 15 (left), 16 (bottom left and
top right), 20, 21, 23 (bottom), 24 (bottom), 37, 38, 42;
Science Photo Library/Gordan Garradd, p. 50; Science
Photo Library/Royal Observatory, Edinburgh, p. 59;
Science Photo Library/TEX Image, p. 53, Science Photo
Library/Hattie Young, p. 40; Juliette Soester, pp. 15
(right), 18, 25, 33, 34, 45, 46.

The publishers have made every effort to contact
copyright holders. However, if any material has been
incorrectly acknowledged, the publishers would be
pleased to correct this at the earliest opportunity.

Websites
Links to appropriate websites are given throughout the
book. Although these were up-to-date at the time of
writing, it is essential for teachers to preview these sites
before using them with pupils. This will ensure that the
web address (URL) is still accurate and the content is
suitable for your needs. We suggest that you bookmark
useful sites and consider enabling pupils to access them
through the school intranet. We are bringing this to your
attention as we are aware of legitimate sites being
appropriated illegally by people wanting to distribute
unsuitable and offensive material. We strongly advise
you to purchase suitable screening software so that
pupils are protected from unsuitable sites and their
material. If you do find that the links given no longer
work, or the content is unsuitable, please let us know.
Details of changes will be posted on our website.

The Bible
Jews call the Bible Tenakh. It is mainly written in Hebrew,
but some parts are in Aramaic, a language similar to
Hebrew. The Tenakh has three parts: Torah (the Five
Books of Moses), Nevi'im (the books of the Prophets) and
Ketuvim (holy writings). In this book, whenever we say
'the Bible' it is the Tenakh that we refer to. For English-
speaking pupils, the quotations are taken from English
translations and can be found in the school Bible.

Tel: 01865 888058   www.heinemann.co.uk

Contents

Introduction to Judaism

In this section you will:

● learn why it is important to study religions so that we have knowledge about the important beliefs that people have and to see how they affect their behaviour

● think about how studying religion helps us to reflect on the big questions of life such as 'What is the purpose of human life?', 'Is there a god?' and 'How do you live a good life?'.

What is Judaism?

Judaism is the name given to the religion followed by Jewish people. They trace its origins back to Abraham, who lived in about 2,000 BCE. Judaism started in the land now called Israel, though from 70 CE most Jews have lived in other countries.

Both Christians and Muslims share many of the stories and teachings of the **Tenakh** (the Hebrew Bible), sharing many beliefs.

The Tenakh has three sections: the **Torah** (the first five books); the **Nevi'im** (prophets); and the **Ketuvim** (holy writings). You will learn more about the Tenakh later in this book.

Judaism is what is called a **monotheistic religion**. That is, Jews believe in only one God. This God was the creator of all things and He is the judge of all people.

Many Jews believe that they have been chosen by God to be His people. He formed a **covenant**, or a promise, with them. He wants them to follow His laws as revealed to Moses. The most important of these laws were the Ten Commandments, which are still the basis for many laws that we have today as well as being important to both Christians and Muslims.

Jews also believe that the nation of Israel is an important part of their story both in the days of the Bible and today.

Joseph on the West End Stage

Moses' story in The Prince of Egypt

Vanessa Feltz

Woody Allen

Stories of importance

Some stories are very important, as they contain ideas about what it means to be a human being and help us to try to answer other big questions that people are interested in.

Art, films and theatre shows are still inspired by stories that were originally told by Jews. Much great music is based on the stories first told by Jewish people and about Jewish people.

Jewish people played an important part in the world. Jonas Salk, who developed the polio vaccine, was Jewish. Shopkeepers such as Michael Marks (of Marks and Spencers) as well as entertainers such as Woody Allen and Barbra Streisand are Jewish.

The writers and thinkers Sigmund Freud and Karl Marx also came from Jewish families.

The book *The Diary of Anne Frank* is about the suffering of the Jews during World War II.

Learning about religion

❶ 'There is no reason to learn about religions, especially the Jewish faith.' What reasons would you give to someone to show that it does matter?

❷ Write a list of the main beliefs of Jews covered in this section. What parts of the Jewish religion do Christians and Muslims share?

❸ Write down the names of some plays, films and musicals that are based on Jewish stories.

Learning from religion

❶ Why are stories so important to people?

❷ Research in more detail one of the Jewish people mentioned and write a talk about their achievements.

Abraham

An easy life?

Perhaps you dream of having an easy life: money, possessions, servants, never having to work unless you wanted to, always free to relax.

Jews believe that there was a man called Abram who lived nearly 4,000 years ago in a city called Haran in modern-day Iraq. He was a wealthy man, married to a woman called Sarai. Aged about 75, Abram and Sarai left the security of the life they knew.

Abram believed that he had been told to go and search for a promised land which he believed God had promised him. Abram was to have the easy life no longer.

Living the easy life

Abram becomes Abraham

The stories about Abram can be found in the early chapters of the book of Genesis in the Jewish scriptures. However, it wasn't long before Abram was given a new name.

In the past, names were much more important than they often are today, as people believed that someone's name could reveal their character or what they were expected to do with their lives.

The stories tell us that Abram was re-named Abraham, a name that meant 'Father of the nations'. His wife Sarai was re-named Sarah because she had laughed when God had told Abraham that she would become a mother to his children. The name 'Sarah' means princess. She was now to be as important as a member of a royal family.

These changes of name showed the beginning of what Jews believe was a **covenant** with Abraham.

For Jews, the covenant is a special promise made by God to people, which shows that He loves them and calls on them to make a response to His love.

Abraham was told that he should make **circumcision** the sign of the covenant. This is where the foreskin of the boy's penis is removed by an operation. This sign of the covenant is still practised by Jews today.

Destruction of Sodom and Gomorrah

Lot was Abraham's nephew. Abraham, Sarah and Lot travelled for many years in the direction of the land they were promised. Lot was Abraham's nephew and decided that he preferred living in a city than the tents of Abraham.

So Lot went to live in Sodom and its neighbouring city of Gomorrah. According to the stories, these two cities were so evil that God decided to destroy them. Abraham prayed to God, asking that if there were some good people they should be rescued. Lot was saved, but the story tells us that Lot's wife was told not to look back at the city. When she did, she was turned into a pillar of salt.

It was a sign to the people that God was interested not in human sacrifices, but in the obedience of the people.

Sacrifice

For many years, Abraham was told by God that he would have a son, but because both he and Sarah were very old, he began to wonder if it would happen. Then Sarah became pregnant. They named their son Isaac.

A few years later, Abraham believed that God had called him to take Isaac and offer him as a sacrifice. Abraham took his son to the mountain and though sad, he prepared himself to kill Isaac. Just as he was about to sacrifice Isaac, he heard the voice of an angel telling him to sacrifice a ram that God had provided instead.

Abraham, about to sacrifice Isaac

Learning about religion

❶ Read the story in Genesis 22 about Abraham and Isaac. Why do you think Jews still find this story important today?

❷ In what ways did Abraham give a good example for Jews of today?

❸ Create a collage based on key moments of Abraham's life. Explain in writing why you have chosen the events in his life that you have.

Learning from religion

❶ Abraham was promised things by God. Discuss with a partner whether or not it is always right to keep your promises. When might it be right not to?

❷ Lot's wife was turned to salt as she looked back, a graphic way of saying that we shouldn't look back on the past. Should we try to forget the past or learn from it?

❸ The Bible stories suggest that Abraham could be a very impatient man. Is patience always a good thing?

Moses

What is leadership?

A leader is a person whom others choose to follow. Leaders are often seen as strong, trustworthy people who have a clear idea of where they want to lead people. For example, Israel's first Prime Minster, David Ben-Gurion, was seen as a leader who had brought his people together in a common purpose – that of forming a new nation.

Moses the leader

Many thousands of years ago, the Jews had been made into slaves by the Egyptians. Although he was Jewish, Moses had been adopted by the Egyptian royal family when he was a baby.

David Ben-Gurion, a modern Moses

However, when he saw a Jewish slave being abused by a slave master, he realized the evil of the society and in anger, killed the slave master. He ran away to the desert, where he became a shepherd and married Zipporah.

While he was living in the desert, Moses had an encounter that led him to feel that God had given him a calling to put things right for the Jews. He saw a bush that seemed to be burning but not being burnt up. He believed that God spoke to him, telling him that he would be responsible for leading his people to freedom.

At first, Moses hesitated. He didn't believe he was a natural leader at all, but eventually he was convinced that he had been called by God to set the Jewish people free and that it was his duty to obey.

Some people believe that Moses saw a bush that really was on fire and heard the voice of God. Others believe that it is a story which shows that God had specially called Moses and that he saw a vision in his mind.

The Passover

Moses went to the Pharaoh of Egypt to ask him to set the Jews free. He told the Pharaoh that God had said, 'Let my people go and worship me in the desert.' The Pharaoh refused, and ten plagues befell Egypt. Moses said that God had sent the plagues because the Pharaoh refused to let the Jewish people go. This made the Jews believe that Moses was their leader who was trusted by God, a role which seemed to be confirmed by the way God had called him at the burning bush. Moses encouraged them to realize that their God was one of justice, who had seen their pain as slaves and was intervening to help them.

The ten plagues sent to Egypt

Despite the plagues, the Pharaoh refused to let the Jews go until the final plague. One night, the Angel of Death visited each house and killed every first-born Egyptian son. The Angel of Death passed over the Jews' houses. They had smeared lamb's blood on their door posts to show they were Jews and so avoid the death of their first-born sons. This is now known as **Pesach** (Passover). The Jews were released from slavery and they escaped from Egypt. This escape from Egypt is called the **Exodus**.

The lawgiver

Moses led the Jewish people for 40 years, and at Mount Sinai he was given the **Torah** – the teachings of God – which included the Ten Commandments. Moses finally led the people to the edge of the land he said that God had promised to them. However, Moses died before he entered the Promised Land.

For many Jews today, Moses is an important role model and an example of a good leader. He is seen as someone who revealed God's purposes by passing on his teachings. He was brave enough to challenge things that were wrong, calling the people to value justice. This is important to Jews today as an example for them to follow.

Learning about religion

❶ Using the information here, explain why Moses is so important to Jewish people.

❷ Do you think the stories about Moses really happened or are they made up to make a point?

❸ Using ICT, design a wall display that shows the key events of the life of Moses. Explain why you think these are key events in the development of Jewish beliefs and why they are important to Jews today.

Learning from religion

❶ a What makes a good leader? Explain why you have chosen these leadership qualities.

b Choose three types of people who lead others and write job descriptions, outlining the leadership qualities they need.

❷ a Moses believed it was important to have rules. Do you think he was right?

b With a partner, discuss the good and bad points of having rules. Make a list of the points you have discussed and briefly explain why you have chosen them.

Elijah

Good anger

Sometimes it is right to get angry. In 1985, Bob Geldof organized the Live Aid concert, which brought together many famous musicians of the time to raise money for the starving people of countries in Africa. During the day, Geldof went on television and was very angry as he did not think people were giving as much as they should. By the end of the event, more than £40 million had been given. How much of this money was given in response to Geldof's anger?

Bob Geldof's anger helped millions through Live Aid

Elijah gets angry

Jews believe that God has sent people throughout their history to pass on His message. These people they call prophets. The prophets both pass on what God says is wrong with the world now, and call on the people to think about the better world that God longs to create, which they can help to bring about if they live obedient lives.

One of the most important of these prophets for Jews is Elijah. Elijah lived during the seventh century BCE at a time when King Ahab and Queen Jezebel ruled Israel. Elijah believed that the King and the Queen often encouraged the people to forsake their worship of God in order to pray to false gods.

Showdown at Mount Carmel

Queen Jezebel had encouraged the people to worship Baal, the chief god of Sidon, the country where she came from. Elijah grew angry at this and believed that God told him to take on the people who were worshipping this god.

There were 450 prophets of Baal, but Elijah was prepared to challenge them all in the name of God. He challenged them to a test of strength on Mount Carmel. Elijah and the prophets of Baal called on their gods to set alight their sacrifices. The prophets of Baal prayed, gashing themselves for their god, but it was Elijah's sacrifice that was consumed by fire, a sign that God was the one true god.

A still small voice

Queen Jezebel wanted Elijah dead after this. Elijah went into hiding, afraid for his life and depressed. He hid in a cave.

Earthquake, wind and fire

The end of the story

Jews believe that Elijah was taken directly to heaven in a chariot, so never died. Many Jews today believe that Elijah has returned to talk to **rabbis** who are especially holy or wise. They also believe that he will return before the **Messiah** comes to Earth.

At the annual celebration of **Pesach**, an empty chair is placed at the table. This is called 'Elijah's chair'.

He saw an earthquake, but this did not seem to him to be from God. Then a fire appeared, but this too did not seem to him to be from God. Then Elijah heard a still, small voice. For Jewish people today, the story shows that God can be known in the small, barely noticeable things of life as well as in the exciting or dangerous things.

Naboth's vineyard

It was the law in Israel at this time that no one could sell any inherited land to the King. One day, King Ahab noticed that his next door neighbour Naboth had a vineyard next to the palace. He asked Naboth if he could buy it so that he could make a vegetable garden. Naboth said that he couldn't go against God, because the law stated that anyone who inherited land could not sell it, even to the King. Naboth said to the King, 'The Lord forbid that I should give you the inheritance of my fathers.'

Ahab went home sad and his wife Jezebel decided to take action. She hired two men to say in public that Naboth had been rude about both the King and God, for which he would have to be put to death.

When this was done, Elijah confronted Ahab, who asked for God's forgiveness.

Learning about religion

❶ Which of the following words match up with what you have read about Elijah? (You must give reasons for your answers). *Weak Strong Caring Thoughtful*

❷ Why do you think Elijah is still so important to Jews today?

❸ Write a poem about the story of Naboth's vineyard. You can find out more details from the story in 1 Kings 21.

Learning from religion

❶ When do you think it might be right to get angry?

❷ What can you do when you think people in power are not doing the right thing?

❸ Find out about the work of development charities like Jewish Care. How do they help modern day Naboths?

Beliefs 1 – God and the covenant

In this section you will:
- understand why the idea of the covenant is so important
- learn why belief in one God is important to Jews.

Promises, promises

A great deal in life depends on promises and trusting others. We feel hurt or disappointed if our friends do not keep their promises. Promises are important at times like marriages too.

Jews believe that God made a promise to care for them and that they are chosen to be His people. They call this promise the covenant. This promise by God should be honoured by Jews trying to live a good life in return.

They believe the first covenant was made with Noah, when God promised never to destroy the whole world again and gave the rainbow as a sign of His love.

Marriage involves making promises

The second covenant was made with Abraham, when God promised to give him many descendants. This was renewed and developed when Moses was given the law (including the Ten Commandments) for the people to follow.

'I am the Lord your God, who brought you out of the land of Egypt, out of the house of slavery, you shall have no other gods before me.'

Exodus 20: 2–3

Many Jews today feel that many of the promises linked to the covenant should now be linked to the state of Israel. The covenant is also regularly reaffirmed by each Jewish family when their sons are circumcised and when their children have a **Bar Mitzvah** or **Bat Mitzvah** ceremony.

Monotheism

'Hear O Israel: The Lord is our God, the Lord alone. You shall love the Lord your God with all your heart, and with all your soul and with all your might.'

Deuteronomy 6: 4

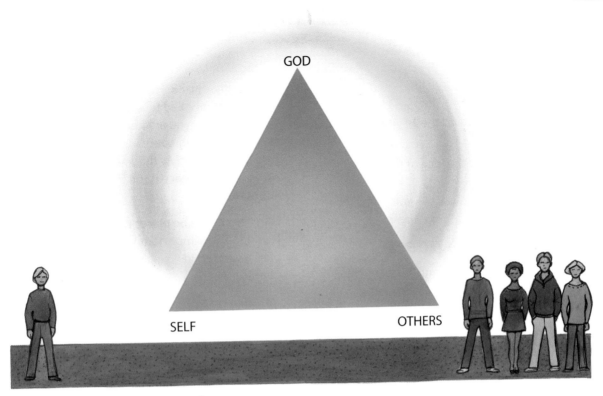

GOD

SELF

OTHERS

Martin Buber's triangle of relationships

This quotation comes from the **Shema**, an important prayer that Jews are encouraged to say daily. It is often written down on scrolls called **mezuzah** and placed in the **tefillin** worn by Jewish men during times of prayer.

Jews were one of the first groups of people to believe in the existence of one God. This idea is called **monotheism**. The one God is the creator and the sustainer of all things that exist. He is the judge, the king of all the universe.

The Jews are told that they must not worship **idols**, statues of gods.

The Jewish thinker Martin Buber wrote a book called *I and Thou*, in which he said that human beings needed to have a relationship with God in order to learn to have proper relationships with each other. As people learn to have relationships with each other, then they also learn to have a relationship with God.

Learning about religion

❶ Why do you think the idea of a covenant is so important to Jews?

❷ Why is the belief in one God good for the Jewish religion?

❸ Draw a diagram to show how the covenant has developed.

Learning from religion

❶ Is it always right to keep your promises? Give reasons for your answers.

❷ How might believing in God affect the way people behave?

Beliefs 2 – shalom

Give me some peace!

There does not seem to be much peace in the world. People fall out in the playground, at home with their relatives and anywhere they get together. We read of wars far away and disputes close to us and wonder if there has ever been any peace at all in the world. Can we ever achieve world peace?

So what is peace?

One dictionary says that peace is 'quiet, mental calm, freedom from war'.

For Jewish people, the idea of peace is very important. The word 'shalom' is used in place of 'Hello ' and 'Goodbye'.

The dove of peace

Peace begins inside you, according to some Jewish teachers. Bad temper, for example, is a sign that inside you are not at peace and that you need to bring peace inside before trying to help others find it. As the Jewish writer Louis Jacobs puts it, 'Peace is the fruit of inner strength.'

Families have to be places where peace can be found too. It is important that husband and wife, parents and child are all trying to live in a peaceful way.

Jewish people do believe, however, that there are times when it is right for people to fight in wars, though they long for a time when wars will be a thing of the past.

Most look to an age of peace. There are many different groups within **Judaism**. They have differing thoughts about their religion. Many people believe that an age of peace will come when God sends his Anointed One (**Messiah**).

The **prophet** Isaiah describes the age of peace in this way:

> The wolf shall live with the lamb,
> The leopard with the kid.
> The calf and the young lion will be together and a little child shall lead them.
> The cow and the bear shall graze, their young shall lie down together; the lion shall eat straw like the ox.
> The nursing child shall play over the hole of the asp and the weaned child shall put its hand on the adder's den. They will not hurt or destroy on all my holy mountain: for the earth will be full of the knowledge of the Lord as the waters cover the sea.
>
> Isaiah 11: 6–9 (Contemporary English Version)

The writer of Psalm 85: 8–9 prayed for this type of peace:

I am listening to what the Lord God is saying;
he promises peace to us, his own people,
if we do not go back to our foolish ways.
Surely he is ready to save those who honour him,
and his saving presence will remain in our land.

Peace is about bringing opposites together, so that they understand each other and do not try to destroy each other. Isaiah shows this by his pictures of nature coming together.

Let the sun rise to light the morning,
Even the purest prayer will not awaken
Bitter tears will not revive will not bring back
Those whose candle was put out and buried in the dust.
Don't say a day will come, seize that day for it is not a dream and in all the squares
Shout out a song for peace!

The song of peace

The Israeli Prime Minister Yitzak Rabin was assassinated in 1995 by some extremists while he was trying to secure peace between the Jews and Palestinians who lived in Israel. In the pocket of the jacket he was wearing was a copy of a poem, written by two Jewish men, called 'The Song of Peace'.

Yitzak Rabin, Prime Minister of Israel, was assassinated for his beliefs

Learning about religion

1 Write a modern version of Isaiah's vision of peace.

2 Jews are not pacifists. Find out what this word means.

3 Find out more about Yitzak Rabin and produce a wall display on his life.

Learning from religion

1 What could you do to make life more peaceful at home, in school and in the world? Draw a spider diagram to show your ideas.

2 'You cannot find peace anywhere except in your self.' What does this mean?

3 Are there times when it is right to fight? Give reasons for your answer, showing that you have thought about it from more than one point of view.

Signs and symbols 1

What is a symbol?

What do the symbols above mean to you?

A symbol is something which represents someone or something else. It might show us feelings, ideas or warnings about its subject. A sign is a mark or a gesture which is used instead of words to put across an important idea.

Symbols are often especially important to religious people because they enable them to think about ideas of great importance, which are often difficult to put into words. Also, symbols can get to mean more over a period of time as they are used in new ways or as people think more about their meaning.

Magen David Adom

The Magen David Adom

No one knows for sure when the Star of David (**Magen David Adom**) became a symbol in the Jewish faith. It may have been an ancient Hindu symbol. An image of this star was found in a synagogue in Capernaum dating from the first century CE.

The Star of David has become an important symbol for the Jewish faith. It recalls how the great Jewish leader, King David, led the nation in the tenth century BCE. From the nineteenth century CE, it has been used as a symbol on synagogues.

When Adolf Hitler came to power in Germany in the 1930s, he ordered that Jews had to wear the Star of David as an armband to identify themselves. This made it easier for the Nazis to arrest them. Hitler and his Nazi Party hated Jews and, by the end of World War II, they had murdered many millions of European Jews. When the Nazis invaded Denmark, the king of the country ordered all his people to wear the Star of David, so that they could smuggle out Jews who lived in the country. This meant that many thousands of Jews escaped death.

After the war, when the country of Israel was established, the Star of David was included in its national flag. It is now seen as a symbol of national pride rather than mass murder.

The menorah

In many religions, light is an important symbol for good overcoming evil. The **menorah**, a six-branched candle-holder, is found in most synagogues. It reminds Jews of how God helped the Israelites when they fought against the evil leader Antiochus Epiphanes who had showed no respect for them or their temple. The story is that a light which should have only burned in the temple for one night went on to burn for eight days. This was a symbol that God was with them and that the defeat of their enemies was assured. A special eight-branched candle-holder, called a **Hanukiah**, is used at the celebration of **Hanukkah** in the winter.

The Hanukiah

Mezuzahs are often found on every door of a Jewish home

The mezuzah

'These commandments which I have given to you this day are to be remembered and taken to heart; repeat them to your children and speak them both inside and outside, when you lie down and when you get up. Bind them as a sign on your hand and wear them as a pendant on your forehead; write them on the door posts of your houses and on your gates.'

Deuteronomy 6: 6–9 (Contemporary English Version)

If you visit Jewish homes today, you will often see small containers like the one above.

In this container is a small scroll that contains a summary of what all Jews should believe. It is fixed to the door frame of every room in the house, except toilets, bathrooms and garages. This is called a **mezuzah** case.

Learning about religion

❶ Write a poem about the way the Star of David has been used over the centuries.

❷ Why do you think light is such an important symbol in many religions?

❸ Why do you think many Jews attach a mezuzah to every door in their homes?

Learning from religion

❶ Find out more about how the people of Denmark helped Jewish people escape when the Nazis occupied the country and write a story about it.

❷ 'The past is the past and should be forgotten.' Why is it important to think about things that happened in the past?

Signs and symbols 2

The tefillin

What matters to you most?

If there were a fire at your house and you could only save one object you owned, what would you choose? It might be a toy or a computer or a photograph that means a lot to you. The things in your room have great importance to you. They have helped to make you the person you are. The objects we own may also help us to become better people.

Tallit

Many Jewish people will wear a **tallit**, a specially made prayer shawl, when they pray. It contains 613 strands, which represent the laws in the **Torah** which they must try to follow.

Tefillin

Many Jewish people also use the **tefillin**. These are small leather boxes which contain the **Shema** prayer. Jews attach them to their head and their arms as a sign of their devotion: their heads and hearts are trying to be obedient to God. The Shema tells Jews to love the Lord with all their head and heart.

The tallit

The kippah

The mikveh is used for ritual bathing

Men visit the mikveh before **Yom Kippur**, an important Jewish festival. Men and women visit the mikveh before the marriage ceremony. Women visit the mikveh after their monthly period has ended or after childbirth.

The idea behind this is that the person must be clean inside as well as outside. By dipping themselves under the water of the mikveh, Jewish people believe they have become purified and fit to talk to God in prayer. The mikveh will remove the consequences of all their bad actions and thoughts.

Kippah

Another distinctive item worn by many Jews is the **kippah**, sometimes called the **yarmulka**. This is a cap that is worn over the head. The kippah is worn as a sign of humility to God. It may have a design such as a Star of David or a **menorah** on it though some children's kippahs may include a non-religious image. The kippah is worn as Jews can pray at any time, and so must have their heads covered in readiness.

The mikveh

The **mikveh** is a special pool where people can immerse themselves to be purified. This is not about physical cleanliness. A Jew would have to be clean outside even before going into the mikveh. It is a way to become spiritually clean.

Learning about religion

❶ Why do you think wearing a kippah might be a sign of humility to God?

❷ Why is a mikveh so important to many Jews?

❸ How might a Jew answer someone who says that religion should not be about what you wear or how you bathe?

Learning from religion

❶ Which item that you own is of most value to you? Is 'precious' the same as 'valuable'?

❷ How could you be humble? Can you ever know if you are?

❸ 'What matters is what is going on in your heart, not the symbols you wear or ritual washing.' What do you think a religious Jew would say to this?

Kosher food

In this section you will:
- learn about the importance of **kosher** food to Jewish people as an expression of their faith
- reflect on how what we eat and how we prepare it reflects our values.

You are what you eat

Food is essential to all of us. For some people, what they eat is of special importance. A vegetarian will try not to eat any meat products, while a vegan will try to avoid any products which come from animals such as milk or cheese. What they eat or refuse to eat demonstrates their beliefs.

Kosher food

Food is very important to Jewish people. **Orthodox Jews** try to follow exactly the laws about what they can and cannot eat from the **Torah**. **Reform Jews** think that the laws were made for a particular time and place.

The word 'kosher' means clean, pure and fit. Kosher food is food that is fit for Jewish people to eat. How do you find out if something is kosher?

In the book of Leviticus, various rules are given. An animal is kosher if it has two characteristics – cloven hooves and it chews the cud (it digests its food through four stomachs). Examples are cows, sheep, goats and deer. The way an animal is killed is very important too, because it has to be killed by a specially trained person, following all the Jewish laws.

Fish are kosher if they have fins and scales, for example cod and trout. Shellfish and oysters would all be considered to be non-kosher. Whale meat, although from a mammal, is treated by the Torah as if it were fish and, therefore, is also not allowed, because whales do not have scales.

Birds such as chicken, duck and turkey are treated as kosher, but birds of prey such as eagles and vultures are seen as non-kosher.

All vegetables and fruit are considered kosher but they must be checked to make sure that small insects or bugs that are not kosher have not infected them. Thorough washing in salt water should make sure vegetables and fruit are fine.

There are many different types of kosher food

Eggs and milk are kosher as long as they come from kosher animals, but all eggs must be checked for little spots of blood, which would make them non-kosher.

One rule that Jews try to follow at home is not to have a meal that has both milk and meat in it. If you had meat for your meal, you could not have custard, which would have milk in it, until a few hours later. In an Orthodox Jewish home, there are often two sinks and two sets of crockery and cutlery for the different types of food.

It is very important to Jews that they know their kosher food is marked as such. You can go into some branches of supermarkets and find specially marked kosher sections. Kosher food will normally have on it a mark of approval, which shows a **rabbi** has approved the item and said that it has been produced in a kosher way.

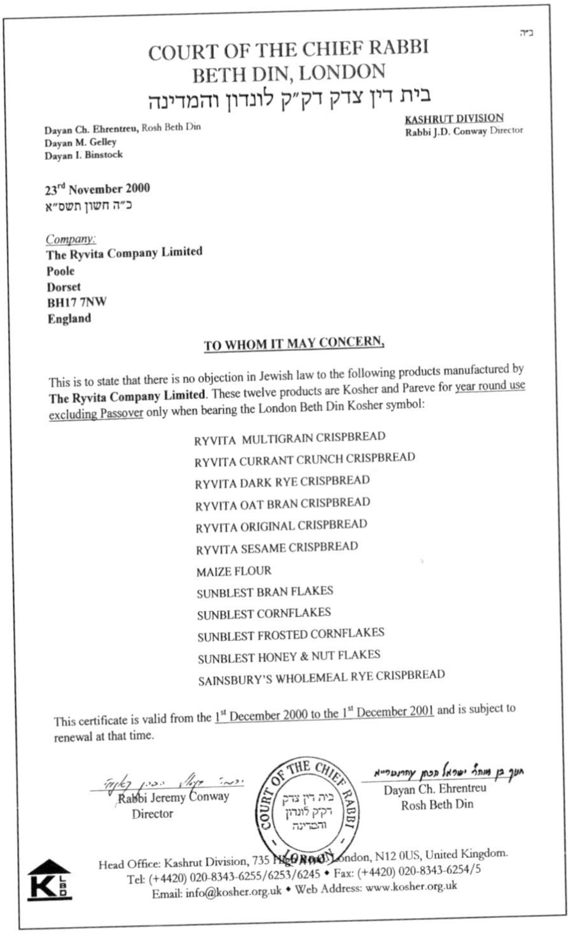

A few years ago, a rumour went round Israel that Coca-Cola was made in a non-kosher way. The board of the company were so alarmed that they allowed a leading rabbi to visit one of the plants where the drink is made. They even let him see the recipe for the drink, which no one outside the company is normally allow to see. Coca-Cola was declared to be kosher.

Sometimes, Jewish people have made sure that they can get to eat kosher food by setting up their own shops to sell it such as kosher butchers. In London's East End, a group of Jews set up a Kosher Luncheon Club to provide good food, specializing in cooking fish dishes. It became popular not just with Jews but also with other people who lived in the area.

COURT OF THE CHIEF RABBI
BETH DIN, LONDON
בית דין צדק דק"ק לונדון והמדינה

Dayan Ch. Ehrentreu, Rosh Beth Din
Dayan M. Gelley
Dayan I. Binstock

KASHRUT DIVISION
Rabbi J.D. Conway Director

23rd November 2000
כ"ה חשון תשס"א

Company:
The Ryvita Company Limited
Poole
Dorset
BH17 7NW
England

TO WHOM IT MAY CONCERN,

This is to state that there is no objection in Jewish law to the following products manufactured by **The Ryvita Company Limited**. These twelve products are Kosher and Pareve for year round use excluding Passover only when bearing the London Beth Din Kosher symbol:

RYVITA MULTIGRAIN CRISPBREAD
RYVITA CURRANT CRUNCH CRISPBREAD
RYVITA DARK RYE CRISPBREAD
RYVITA OAT BRAN CRISPBREAD
RYVITA ORIGINAL CRISPBREAD
RYVITA SESAME CRISPBREAD
MAIZE FLOUR
SUNBLEST BRAN FLAKES
SUNBLEST CORNFLAKES
SUNBLEST FROSTED CORNFLAKES
SUNBLEST HONEY & NUT FLAKES
SAINSBURY'S WHOLEMEAL RYE CRISPBREAD

This certificate is valid from the 1st December 2000 to the 1st December 2001 and is subject to renewal at that time.

Rabbi Jeremy Conway
Director

Dayan Ch. Ehrentreu
Rosh Beth Din

Head Office: Kashrut Division, 735 High Road, London, N12 0US, United Kingdom.
Tel: (+4420) 020-8343-6255/6253/6245 • Fax: (+4420) 020-8343-6254/5
Email: info@kosher.org.uk • Web Address: www.kosher.org.uk

A kosher food certificate

Learning about religion

❶ Why do Orthodox Jews still believe that it is important to follow the kosher food laws?

❷ Design a leaflet or a poster to explain what the kosher laws are to children.

❸ Which of the following are kosher? Give reasons for your answer. Potato, smoky bacon crisps, fresh orange juice, rabbit pie.

Learning from religion

❶ Many people think that what they eat matters. What reasons might they give to explain this? Do you think what you eat matters? Give your reasons.

❷ Canteens in schools and offices need to cater for people with many different dietary requirements. How could they ensure they provide the very best for their customers?

Worship at home 1 – Shabbat

In this section you will:
- reflect on the need that human beings have for rest and reflection
- learn about the importance of the day of **Shabbat** to Jews.

Holy days and holidays

We all need to have some rest and relaxation at times. Originally, many times of rest were linked with holy days, but now any time off is called a holiday.

Weekends have become an important time to many people, when they can rest from the work they do during the week.

The idea of rest is very important to Jews, as a time to remember God's creation of the world and as a time to rest. It is called Shabbat in Hebrew (the Sabbath). For **Orthodox Jews**, it begins at sunset on Friday night and ends at sunset on Saturday. For **Reform Jews**, Shabbat will begin and end at the same time on Friday and Saturday (normally at 6pm on Friday to 6pm on Saturday).

Why is there Shabbat?

'On the seventh day, having finished all his work, God blessed the day and made it holy, because it was the day when he finished all his work of creation.'

Genesis 2: 2–3

'Remember to keep the Sabbath day holy. You have six days to labour and do all your work; but the seventh day is the Sabbath of the Lord your God; that day you must not do any work, neither you nor your son nor your daughter, your slave or slave-girl, your cattle or the foreigner living with you, for the Lord made the heavens and the earth in six days, the sea and all that is in them, and on the seventh day he rested. Therefore the Lord blessed the Sabbath day and called it holy.'

Exodus 20: 8–11

In the book of Deuteronomy, the Israelites are also reminded that they should keep the Sabbath in thanks for the way God rescued them from Egypt.

A family celebrates Shabbat

Shabbat today

Before Shabbat begins, the house will be cleaned and prepared. All shopping necessary for food during Shabbat will be done the day before. The table will be set, best clothes will be put on. Some Jews will go to the **synagogue** before returning from work, some will go to the synagogue on the morning of Shabbat.

Just before Shabbat, the mother of the household lights two candles and says a special prayer to welcome the beginning of the time of rest. The blessing is for her family and the candles are symbols of the joy and peace she has asked God to bring to her home.

The family will sit down for a meal together, which will include the **Kiddush** blessing, where the father takes a cup of wine and asks for blessings over the family.

There are two plaited loaves called **challot** (singular **challah**), which remind Jews of the **manna**, the special bread that God provided in the desert when they had escaped from Egypt. This was provided so that they did not have to work on the Sabbath day. The father will take a piece of the challot and dip it in salt, to remind the family of the destruction of the temple in Jerusalem.

There is no work done during Shabbat and anything that encourages others to work is avoided as far as possible. For some Jews, this means that even turning on a light must be avoided, although some have automatic timers for ovens and lights.

Towards the end of Shabbat, a spice box is handed round and a plaited candle is lit. The spice box is a symbol to say that the hope is for a good new week and the candle reminds Jews that God's first act in the first week was to make light. This ceremony is called the **Havdalah**. There are more blessings:

- over a cup of wine

- over the spices to show that the spiritual part of the week has gone and the 'ordinary' day is about to begin

- over the candle-flame to show that Jews may once again light a fire and finally a blessing to thank God for providing a holy day of rest.

A spice box

Learning about religion

❶ What reasons according to the Bible is Shabbat to be kept?

❷ Write about three symbolic things that take place around the time of Shabbat.

❸ Why do you think the destruction of the Temple is remembered at the Shabbat meal?

Learning from religion

❶ Do you think that we need a day of rest? Give reasons for your answer.

❷ How could you bring peace to the next week?

Worship at home 2 – prayer

In this section you will:

- learn about the importance of worship at home to Jewish people
- reflect on how a family doing things together helps bring them closer together.

Worship begins at home

Jews believe that it is good for a family to pray together as it helps bring them together, and makes them more aware of each others' needs.

At many festivals, worship begins in the home and then continues in the **synagogue**. At **Shabbat**, many prayers are said in both places.

Women, who may not pray aloud in the synagogue, often lead the prayers at home.

Why pray?

Worship at home is very important to Jews because the home and family life are seen as very important parts of life. Jews believe that they are in a special relationship with God called the **covenant** and that this means they should deepen that relationship by prayer, both individually and in groups.

It is very important that a Jew makes sure that their intention behind a prayer is good. Jews call this intention **Kavanah** and if it is for an evil or selfish purpose, they believe they will be judged on that.

There are many reasons why Jewish people think it is important to pray. First and foremost, they believe that prayer will deepen their relationship with God, the God who has been with their people for centuries and who made a covenant to love them.

Reading the Siddur

Jewish people may also pray because they need to ask for something or on behalf of someone in need.

Another reason to pray is to thank God for the blessings that He has given to them as individuals and as a people. They worship God because they believe that He created the world and rescued the people of Israel from the slavery they knew in Egypt.

Types of prayer

Most Jews will use a prayer book called a **Siddur**, which contains prayers they can use at home or at the synagogue services of prayer held during the day.

The prayers begin with the **Shema** (see page 10). This is followed by the **Amidah** or the eighteen benedictions ('benediction' means 'blessing'). They always conclude:

'Blessed are thou, O Lord Our God, King of the Universe.'

Many of the phrases used in the prayers come from the Bible, such as this one from the book of the prophet Isaiah:

'Holy, holy, holy is the Lord of hosts,
The whole earth is full of your glory.'

Isaiah 6: 3

Most of the time, Jews pray standing up, but they may bow as they refer to God the King. On certain high holy days, such as **Yom Kippur** (see pages 32–3), **Orthodox Jews** may kneel as a sign of humility before God. For prayer, Jewish men and some women wear the prayer robe or **tallit**, and men usually wear a **kippah** and **tefillin** (see page 16).

Ready for prayer

Learning about religion

❶ Like people from many religions, Jews pray for many different reasons. List three reasons why Jews might pray. Do you think one is more important than another? Give reasons for your answer.

❷ How might prayer help a Jewish family to come together?

❸ Research Shabbat in more detail and devise a wall display to show its most important points.

Learning from religion

❶ 'Prayer is a waste of time.' How might a Jewish person answer this? What do you think?

❷ 'What matters most in prayer is your intention, not your actions while you are praying.' Do you agree?

Worship in the synagogue

In this section you will:

- learn about why the **synagogue** is an important place for Jewish people
- learn what happens there
- reflect on the importance of special buildings to groups of people.

Places that matter

We all have places that matter to us more than others. It might be the place where we were born or where we live. Or it might be a place where we have gone on holiday.

For Jews, there have always been special places to meet with God. Until the first century CE, they worshipped in a temple in Jerusalem and in local places of worship. When the temple was destroyed, the synagogue became the most important place to worship God.

The synagogue

The word 'synagogue' means a place of meeting or assembly. The Hebrew for this is **Bet ha Knesset**. Some American Jews call their synagogues temples in memory of the temple in Jerusalem. Other names for the synagogues include the House of Study and the House of Prayer.

What do you see inside in a synagogue?

There are some things that you will find in any synagogue, be it of the Orthodox or Reform tradition.

In every synagogue, there is a large cupboard called **Aron Hakodesh** (the **Ark**). In this are stored the scrolls of the **Torah** and other holy writings.

The Torah scrolls are taken from the Ark

The scrolls can be covered by a piece of cloth, which is normally decorated or sometimes they are stored in wooden cylinders. The Torah scrolls also have a small shield hung over them as well as a pointer called a **yad**. The shield represents the breastplate worn by priests in the ancient temple. The yad is used to point to the words on the scrolls when reading during services.

There is also a set of bells placed on top to act as a crown, because the Jews believe that the Torah is the teaching of the great king that is God.

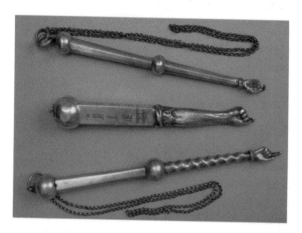

Yad pointers come in a variety of styles

Inside a synagogue

Many families will pay to have new copies of the scrolls presented to the synagogue to remember an important event in their lives such as a birth, marriage or death.

Above the Ark is the **Ner Tamid**, the eternal light which burns here as a sign of God's eternal **covenant**. Also above the Ark are two tablets, reminding the congregation of the Ten Commandments given to Moses.

In the centre of the synagogue is the **bimah**. It is here that the scrolls are taken to be read from a reading desk. In Orthodox synagogues, it is normally the **rabbi** who will read the **sidra**, the portion of the Torah set for the **Shabbat** service. Synagogues also have a **cantor**, who leads the sung parts of the service.

In an Orthodox synagogue, the rabbi, the cantor and the **wardens** have special seats. Wardens are people who have been chosen by other members to help people find seats and to make sure that there are no disturbances to the service.

Sometimes families pay an annual sum to belong to the synagogue in order to support its work. Important events in family life, such as **Bar** and **Bat Mitzvah** and weddings, will take place in the synagogue. Subscriptions will pay for the upkeep of the building and pay the salary of the rabbi and anyone else who works full time for the synagogue.

There are some very important differences between Orthodox and Reform synagogues, which we will look at in our next section.

Learning about religion

❶ What reasons might a Jew give for going to the synagogue?

❷ Why do you think the Ark in a synagogue is so important? Give reasons for your answer.

❸ Do you think families should pay a subscription to belong to the synagogue?

Learning from religion

❶ 'You can be religious without other people about.' How might a Jew answer this? What would you say?

❷ 'You don't need to go to a synagogue to be a Jew.' Why might a Jewish person disagree with this statement? Why might another Jewish person agree? What do you think? Give reasons for your answer.

Orthodox and Reform synagogues

In this section you will:

● learn about the differences between the Orthodox and Reform synagogues

● reflect on the differences there can be within a religion.

Tradition or change?

We live in a society that is changing all the time. Not so long ago, computers could occupy entire rooms, now we have little computers inside watches. The Internet has led to great changes in understanding the world around us. Women can now vote and have jobs when in the past they were not allowed to do so. But is all change for the good and is it right to sometimes resist change?

One of the most difficult questions that religious people have to face is whether they keep their religion as it was when it first began, or whether they change things as people reflect on what is going on in society.

Jewish groups

The Jewish community has a number of different groups within it. There are secular Jews, who are not religious but who acknowledge the importance of their background. **Ashkenazim** are Jews who trace their ancestors back to Eastern Europe whilst **Sephardim** come from Spain and North Africa. Two of the largest groups are **Orthodox Jews** and **Reform Jews**.

Orthodox Jews want things to remain unchanged because they believe that keeping traditions, teachings and festivals shows that they are still relevant today, and there is no need to change. They believe these things will always be right. They believe that the teachings in the **Torah** are timeless and will always need to be applied today. They look forward to the coming of a **Messiah** who will bring peace to the world.

Reform Jews believe that teachings were expressed and provided in the way that people needed them when they first received them. They believe that you can take unchanging principles but apply them in new ways. So, for example, it was necessary to keep **kosher** food in the days of the Torah, but with modern methods of storing and preserving food, we do not need to be quite so restrictive. Reform Jews believe that it is the duty of every Jew to try to bring peace into the world, rather than wait for a Messiah figure who will bring a golden age with them.

The different **synagogues** show some of the differences between Orthodox and Reform Jews. The most obvious is that in an Orthodox synagogue, the men sit on the ground floor and the women and children (including any boys who have not yet had their **Bar Mitzvah**) sit separately. In the Reform synagogue, the men, women and their children all sit together.

In an Orthodox synagogue, the **rabbi** is always male whereas in the Reform synagogues, the rabbi can be either male or female.

The times at which **Shabbat** begins also differs between the Orthodox and the Reform traditions. The Orthodox believes that Shabbat always begins at sunset on Friday, even if this varies throughout the year. The Reform say that Shabbat should be observed from 6pm on Friday onwards.

Inside an Orthodox synagogue

A woman rabbi reading the Torah in a Reform synagogue

The service in an Orthodox synagogue in the United Kingdom is in Hebrew apart from prayers for the royal family and the state of Israel. In a Reform synagogue, much more of the service is in English.

There are differences in the music used in worship in the synagogue too. In an Orthodox synagogue, the choir is male only and no instruments are used in the worship. In the Reform synagogue, the choir will be both male and female. An organ may be used to accompany the singing of the congregation.

Every synagogue has to have a minimum of ten people, called a **minyan**, in order for worship to take place. In an Orthodox synagogue, this number has to be made up from men who have had their Bar Mitzvah. In the Reform synagogues, the minyan can consist of both men and women.

The length of synagogue services are also very different. On the morning of Shabbat, the Orthodox Jews meet at 9am for about three hours whereas the Reform Jews meet at about 11am for an hour and a half.

Both types of synagogue will have services of prayer throughout the week for the faithful to attend. They also provide places where the young can be taught about the faith and the traditions and history of the Jewish people.

Learning about religion

❶ What are the most important differences between Orthodox and Reform synagogues?

❷ 'Religions must always try to up date themselves.' How would an Orthodox Jew reply to this?

❸ Design a leaflet to explain what Reform Jews believe.

Learning from religion

❶ 'You cannot change traditions without losing the meaning of the religion.' What do you think?

❷ 'Men and women are different and they need to be treated in different ways.' Organize a class debate on this topic.

The Written Torah

In this section you will:

- learn about some of the important books, scriptures and holy writings of Judaism that help Jewish people in the decisions they face in their life and give them a source for their beliefs

- reflect on how books shape our own lives.

The power of books

In his novel *Fahrenheit 451*, the science fiction writer Ray Bradbury imagines a time when a government has taken over that is so afraid of the power of books to make people think and question the way things are that they organize book burnings.

Books can change the way we think or feel about the world. They can be very powerful items.

Scriptures

Scriptures, the writings of a religion, are very important to religious people. They contain the key stories, accounts of important events and teachings that are central to the belief. They help people to live according to their beliefs by giving rules and instructions.

For Jews, the holy writings, especially the **Torah**, reveal in their words and stories the way God would like people to live. They show His **covenant**, His promise to the Jews always to be their God.

Reading the Torah at the Western Wall

The Torah

'Blessed are thou O Lord God of the Universe who has chosen us from all people and has given us thy Torah.'

This prayer of blessing is said before the reading of the Torah in the **synagogue**. The Torah is the name given to the first five books of the Jewish scriptures: Genesis, Exodus, Leviticus, Numbers and Deuteronomy. The word 'Torah' comes from a Hebrew word that can mean direction, instruction or teachings – all of them are true in order to fully understand the importance of the book.

The Torah contains the stories of creation, the calling of Abraham, and the stories of Isaac, Jacob and Joseph. Above all, the story of Moses and the escape from Egypt is right at the heart of it all. The Torah contains the 613 **mitzvot** (rules) that were given to Moses, the first ten being what are now called the Ten Commandments.

There are 248 positive mitzvot and 365 negative mitzvot. Some prayer shawls have 613 strands to remind Jews of these rules.

Of course, it is difficult to remember all the rules. What some of the rules teach is not always clear. Some of the meanings of the rules in the Torah have been discussed by many **rabbis** and other scholars over the years debating what they mean. One such scholar was Hillel, who wrote the following in the first century CE:

'What is hateful to you, do not do to your neighbour. That is the whole of the Torah. All else is commentary.'

Many Jewish children will attend a **cheder**, a special school to help them to understand the teachings of the Torah. In their twenties, some of them may attend a **Yeshiva**, a college where they will study the holy writings in depth for three or four years.

Orthodox Jews believe that every word in the Torah comes directly from God and will remain in force for ever. Other Jews, such as **Reform Jews**, believe that you have to interpret the rules in line with what we know about the world today. For this reason, some Jews might not observe the **kosher** food laws and see no problem with a woman becoming a rabbi, while others Jew might think this was wrong.

The Nevi'im and Ketuvim

The Torah is one part of what Jews refer to as the written Torah. The other two parts are called the **Nevi'im** and the **Ketuvim**. The Nevi'im are the writings of the prophets and include some of the historical books about the Kingdom of Israel. The Ketuvim are the writings of the people of Israel, such as the Psalms, the Proverbs and the book of Job. Together, these three sections are known as the **Tenakh**, the collection of writings that Christians call the Old Testament.

Learning about religion

❶ Draw a diagram to explain the make up of the holy writings that form the written Torah.

❷ What do you think Rabbi Hillel meant by what he said that all you had to do was avoid what is hateful to your neighbour to do all the Torah?

❸ Explain the different views about the Torah that you can find amongst Jewish people.

Learning from religion

❶ Can books written thousands of years ago still be relevant to help us live our lives now? Give reasons.

❷ How have you and other people been influenced by books and films? Have they changed the way you look at the world in any ways?

The Oral Torah

In this section you will:

● learn about the importance of the **Mishnah**, the **Talmud** and other Jewish writings found outside the **Torah** to Jewish life and experience

● reflect on how you make principles from other times and places relevant to life now.

How is law made?

If you were to go into a court, you would soon find out that the law is something that is always changing and developing. Laws are passed by parliament and the courts' first job is to uphold these laws. The courts, however, often have to apply the way the laws work to particular cases. The courts also have to consider what the consequences of the law might be to areas that the lawmakers did not first think about.

Jewish scriptures could be said to be made in a similar way. First, the **Tenakh** writings, especially the Torah, are referred to, but where do you go if those writings do not talk about the issue you are concerned about or if what they say is hard for you to understand? For Jews, other writings which interpret and apply the laws are very important. They refer to the Written Torah (the Tenakh) and the Oral Torah, formed by thinking over how to apply the principles.

A law court in action

The Mishnah

The translation of the Hebrew word 'Mishnah' means 'to repeat, to study'. The Mishnah came to be written down in 200 CE. It deals with issues such as the times to plant seeds and how to observe **Shabbat** and other festivals. It has sections on marriage, divorce, buying and selling, sacrifices and what makes you impure at worship, and is the written version of the Oral Torah.

All of these sayings were collected by **Rabbi** Judah the Prince, who took great care in editing them all.

The Talmud

The Talmud took more than 800 years to complete and represents the teachings and ideas of at least 2000 rabbis and other Jewish religious teachers. It contains long stories, designed to help people understand the way they should live called **Agadah**. It also has some reflections on how laws could be applied to new problems, which are called **Halakhah**.

The Talmud contains some wise and thoughtful sayings such as the following:

'The health of the body depends upon the teeth.'

'Breakfast is the most important meal of the day.'

'Charity knows no race or creed.'

Midrash

As well as the Mishnah and the Talmud, Jews often refer to writings called **Midrashim**. These are writings based on passages in the Tenakh such as the stories about Moses, Jonah, David or Noah. They are an attempt to find the meaning of all the passages of the Tenakh, which may not necessarily be immediately obvious.

How are these holy writings used today?

The Talmud, the Mishnah and the Midrashim are used to help understand the ideas of the written Torah and to find ways of working out what they mean in practice. They may also be used to help in the judgements of the special Rabbinical courts called the **Bet Din** on such issues as whether a divorce can be granted or who inherits from a will.

Learning about religion

1. Give two ways in which laws are made. What problems might result if laws are made in these ways?

2. Why do you think Jewish people felt they needed the Mishnah and the Talmud?

3. 'It is impossible to apply the Torah today.' How might a Jew answer that statement?

Learning from religion

1. Choose one of the quotations from the Talmud. Ask two people to speak for the statement and two to speak against it. Then vote for and against the statement.

2. 'It is your conscience that is the best thing to help you live a good life, not a book.' How would a Jewish person answer this? What do you think? Give reasons for your answer.

Festivals 1 – Yom Kippur

In this section you will:

- learn about the importance of **Yom Kippur** to Jewish people
- reflect on whether it is always right to forgive other people
- reflect on what it means to accept forgiveness for yourself.

Times to celebrate, times to think

Festivals are very important times for religious people because they enable them to reflect on important teachings and events of the faith they follow. As we look at festivals, we can also learn from them about some answers to some of the most important questions people ask about how we behave and what matters most in life.

I can't forgive myself...

Have you ever done anything that you felt so guilty about that you found it hard to forgive yourself? Perhaps you said something cruel or did something nasty, perhaps you just forgot to do something you know you should have done.

We all need to forgive ourselves sometimes

Jews believe that justice and mercy go together. If you do something wrong, then it is right to ask for forgiveness or mercy as well as to try to put the matter right in a practical way if necessary.

At the time of Yom Kippur, Jews especially remember their need to be forgiven by God and other human beings.

What is Yom Kippur?

Yom Kippur means 'The Day of **Atonement**'. Atonement means making up for things you have done wrong and making peace with the people you have upset. On this day of atonement Jews try to become at peace with God. In order to get to this point, you will need to ask for forgiveness and accept there are things about yourself that will have to be changed in order to make this possible.

Rosh Hashanah is Jewish New Year, and it falls in September or October. At this time Jews remember God as creator. For ten days after New Year, the 'Days of Return', Jews make an effort to put right things that they have done wrong. Then on Yom Kippur, God is remembered as judge.

For about a month before Yom Kippur, the **shofar** is blown in the **synagogue**. This is a ram's horn and its sound calls people to think through where they need to ask forgiveness. In the past, rams were sacrificed in the Jewish temple as one way of showing a determination to **repent** (to say sorry and try to live in the way God wants).

'On the tenth day of the seventh month, you must fast.'

Leviticus 16: 29

The day before Yom Kippur, Jews have to prepare themselves. They will use the **mikveh**, a special bath used for religious purposes to purify themselves. They will then have a meal before beginning the twenty-five hour **fast**.

To fast is to give up food for religious reasons.

'To know what it is to be hungry, even for a single day, encourages pity for the hungry, the oppressed and the unfortunate.'

Jewish thinker, Louis Jacobs

It is important that a Jewish person is sincere about the wrong they have done, and that they become committed to living a good life, honouring God.

On Yom Kippur, Jews avoid sexual intercourse. They do not wear leather shoes, as people used to think that wearing leather shoes was a way of showing off their wealth.

Jews spend the day after in prayer and settle any disputes that they have with other people.

At the end of the day of Yom Kippur, there is a service in the synagogue. The doors of the **Ark** are flung open, a way of saying that God wants to accept them. The shofar is blown again to signify the end of the day.

Blowing the shofar

Learning about religion

❶ Write down the meanings of atonement, fasting and repentance.

❷ Draw a diagram showing the most important things that happen at the time of Yom Kippur.

❸ Why do you think many Jews feel that Yom Kippur is the holiest day of the year?

Learning from religion

❶ Is it always right to forgive other people? Give reasons for your answer.

❷ What would you find most difficult to give up for a day? Why would you find this difficult?

❸ 'If Yom Kippur really worked, it wouldn't need to happen every year.' How would you answer this statement?

Festivals 2 – Purim

In this section you will:

- learn about why the festival of **Purim** is so important to Jews
- reflect on how important it is to be true to yourself.

The festival story

You can find the story of Purim in the book of Esther in the Jewish scriptures.

A long time ago, the Jews were invaded by the Persians, who took some of them from Israel to their capital, Susa. Two of the people who went to live there were Esther and her cousin Mordecai.

The King of Persia was called Xerxes. One day, Xerxes ordered his wife, Queen Vashti to come to a party. She refused. The King felt humiliated by his wife's refusal to do as she was told and his advisers suggested that he quietly divorce her before people in the Persian Empire heard of what she had done.

Jewish children performing a Purim play

The King needed a new Queen and so his prime minister, Haman, helped to organize a search for a replacement. Haman hated Jews, especially Mordecai whom he hated more than anyone else.

Many girls were taken to the King's palace for him to choose from. One of them was Esther. Mordecai told her that she must not let the King know she was a Jew.

King Xerxes saw the suggested replacements to Queen Vashti and decided that Esther was the most beautiful he saw. They were married.

Haman continued to plot against Jews, trying to influence the King. Haman had drawn lots (called purim) to see what day the murder of Mordecai and the other Jews should be.

Mordecai heard that Haman was planning to kill him so he asked Esther to go and visit the King in his private chambers at night. This was very dangerous, as it could be punishable by death. Esther was not afraid. She told the King that she was a Jew and that Haman had been plotting to kill Mordecai and her people.

The King was angry with Haman and invited him to dinner. During dinner, the King told Haman that he knew of his plan and that Esther was Jewish. He ordered the palace guard to go and hang Haman on the gallows he had had built for Mordecai. The Jews were saved.

After this, the King issued an order throughout the Persian Empire that Jews should be allowed to defend themselves against attack and that any one who had plotted with Haman was to be arrested and punished.

Purim today

At the festival of Purim today, the story of Esther is read at sunset and into the next day in the synagogue. People, especially children, often dress up and perform Purim plays based on the story.

The telling of the story is a bit like a pantomime, because whenever Haman's name is mentioned, children boo loudly, stamp their feet or wave a rattle known as a **greggar** to try and stop his name from being heard.

The **Talmud** instructs people that they should give gifts at the time of Purim. It is now customary to give at least two items of food to friends (though some people send a gift such as a book).

Most **Orthodox Jews** believe that the events of Purim happened as the Book of Esther records them, but many **Reform Jews** are less sure because there is no other historical record of the story happening. However, both are agreed that this story shows how God saves those who trust in Him.

Learning about religion

❶ Why do you think Purim is still an important festival to Jews today?

❷ Does it matter if the story of Purim didn't happen as the book of Esther suggests? Give reasons for your answer and show that you have thought about it from more than one point of view.

❸ Draw a picture to illustrate the story of Esther.

Learning from religion

❶ Haman tried to get rid of the Jews because he was racist. What do you think causes racism? Give as many reasons as possible.

❷ Is revenge ever right? Why might religious people think it wrong?

❸ In the story, Esther learns that it is important to be true to yourself. What might this mean to you?

The Western Wall

The journey of life

Many people see life as being like a journey. Along the journey we meet new people, see new things and learn things from others. But is it a journey with a point or a destination, or is it just the fun of travelling that makes things worthwhile?

For religious people, making a journey to a place of great importance to their faith will help them to focus on their faith and their own development in understanding.

Tale of a temple

When the Jews first began worshipping God, they would gather rocks in the desert to mark places. By the time of Moses, worship took place in a large tent called a tabernacle.

In the centre of the tabernacle was a box called the **Ark of the Covenant**. According to Jewish tradition this contained the Spirit of God and also the two tablets of stone that Moses had been given with the Ten Commandments on them.

According to the **Tenakh**, King David made Jerusalem the capital city of Israel and decided that a temple should be built there. But it was actually built by David's son, Solomon.

The temple was to become a very important centre of the Jewish religion for a number of reasons. First, it contained the Ark of the Covenant in a special area called the Holy of Holies. This place was so sacred that priests could only visit it once a year in rotation. Secondly, it was in the temple that the animals were sacrificed to God as a way of saying sorry for the evil things the people had done.

The first temple was built by King Solomon. This was destroyed by invasion and re-built. The second temple was destroyed by a later invasion. At the time of Jesus, a new temple had just been completed. Although local **synagogues** had begun to develop, most Jews still tried to visit the temple.

In 66 CE, the Jews rebelled against the Romans and in 70 CE, the Romans set fire to the city. They destroyed all of the temple, apart from the outside Western Wall.

The Western Wall today

The Western Wall remains in the centre of Jerusalem, an important symbol of the temple that one day some Jews hope will be re-built on that site. Today, the Western Wall is an important place to go and pray.

The Western Wall is seen as an open air synagogue. Men and women stand separately (as is the case in some Orthodox synagogues). Men wear **kippah** to cover their heads whilst praying. Some parents may hold their son's **Bar Mitzvah** there.

There is a tradition to write a prayer on a piece of paper and then place it in the wall. Many Jews do this. The wall has to be regularly emptied due to the amount of requests placed in it.

When the state of Israel was formed in 1948, the part of Jerusalem the Western Wall was in lay in the Arab country of Jordan. Above the wall is a hill where the Muslim holy places of the Dome of the Rock and the Black Mosque can be found. In 1967, Israel and Jordan fought a war which led to Israel capturing the area around the Western Wall, making it easier for Jews to visit this important site.

Learning about religion

❶ Draw a diagram to show the development of where Jews have worshipped, with notes explaining about the important aspects of each place.

❷ Why is the Western Wall still important to Jews today?

❸ Find out more about the area around the Western Wall, especially the Muslim sites of the Dome of the Rock and the Black Mosque. You should prepare notes to give a short talk on the area around the Western Wall.

Learning from religion

❶ Which places are important to you? Give reasons for your answer.

❷ What prayer would you write on a piece of paper and insert in the Western Wall? Give reasons for your answers.

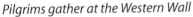

Pilgrims gather at the Western Wall

Masada

Dying for what you believe in?

There are many examples in history when people have preferred to die rather than give up their religion or where they have died in order to try to save their nation from attack.

Masada made an impressive fortress

To some, dying for a cause seems an extreme thing to do. To others, it seems natural that if something means so much to you, then you would be willing to stand up for the principle, even if it cost you your life.

Masada today

Masada is a hill, 150 metres high, in the middle of the desert near the Dead Sea in Israel. Temperatures can reach well over 40 degrees centigrade. To reach the top of Masada, most people use the cable-cars rather than try to walk up the rocky path.

Archaeologists uncovered the site of Masada in the 1960s and since then, it has become both a place for the tourist and the pilgrim to visit.

Soldiers in the Israeli army have to run from the bottom of the hill in full kit, as part of their training. When they reach the top, they promise that 'Masada will not fall again'.

Why Masada became important

In 4 BCE, King Herod the Great built a palace on the top of Masada. After his death, the Romans took control of it for a time.

In 66 CE, a group of Jews known as the **Zealots** started a civil war against the Romans. One part of this group captured Masada and made it their base.

In the autumn of 72 CE, the Romans decided to deal with the Zealots of Masada. On Masada, the Zealots were able to grow food and they had storerooms cut out of the rock which could store enough water and grain to supply their needs for many years if necessary. How could the Romans reach the top of the steep rock?

The Romans stormed Masada

The Romans set up camps around the base of Masada and put up a series of fences which meant no-one could get in or go out without permission. They also brought a large number of slaves to build a huge rocky pathway up to the fort the Zealots held. After many months of building, the Romans reached the top.

The leader of the Zealots was Eleazar, who told them that it was better to die as free people than submit to the slavery the Romans would bring. It was decided to set the fortress alight and then to choose people to end the lives of all the Zealots. Ten men were selected to kill the 960 people who lived there.

Not all of them died. Two women and five children hid themselves in order to avoid being killed. According to a historian called Josephus, they gave an account of what had happened to the Romans when they broke through the walls and found their enemies dead.

The Romans were impressed by the action of the Zealots, for they too believed that it was better to die than to suffer dishonour. It seemed that in some way it was really the Zealots who had won the battle of Masada.

Learning about religion

❶ Why do you think the soldiers of the Israeli army make the vow 'Masada shall not fall again'?

❷ Imagine that you were one of the survivors of Masada. Write an account of why the people chose to kill themselves. Remember to include what Eleazar had said to them.

❸ Why do you think modern Jews think of Masada as a special place?

Learning from religion

❶ Do you think the people on Masada were right to do what they did? Give reasons for your answer.

❷ 'The people on Masada should have fought until the last person. Suicide was a coward's way out.' What do you think a modern Jewish person might say to this? What might your answer be? Give reasons for what you think.

❸ 'A person who has not found a cause to die for, has not found a reason to live.' (Martin Luther King) Do you agree? Give reasons for your answer.

Circumcision – sign of the covenant

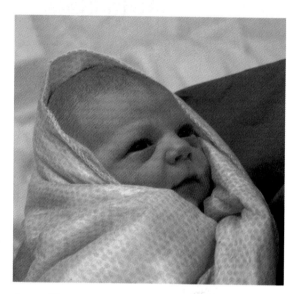

A new life

Stages of life

Do you remember when you were born? Probably not, but there are people who love you who do. Do you remember when you left primary school? There was probably a final assembly, as a way of saying goodbye to where you have been as well as preparing you for the future.

Religious people think that it is important to acknowledge the important moments of life. They believe that it is important to have a ceremony to help people in the new stage of their lives such as a baptism or a wedding. These special ceremonies are called **rites of passage**. These ceremonies reveal the ideas and teachings of the religion.

The covenant promise

Both girls' and boys' births are acknowledged by Jews. Boys have a special ceremony to welcome them into the Jewish community. This is called circumcision.

Circumcision is the practice of removing the foreskin from a boy's penis. Although circumcision existed a long time before the Jewish faith and is sometimes performed on non-Jewish boys, for Jews it is a very important sign of their relationship with God called the **covenant**.

Jewish people call circumcision **Brit Milah**, 'the covenant of circumcision'. One of the prayers used at the ceremony shows how important it is, because it links back to the first circumcision which Abraham practised as a sign of the covenant with God.

'Praised be thou, O Lord our God, ruling spirit of the Universe who has commanded us to enter into the covenant of our father Abraham.'

Prayer from the Brit Milah Service

Circumcision always takes place on the eighth day after the mother has given birth, after she has visited the **mikveh** for her purification.

Circumcisions can happen either at the **synagogue** or in the home of the family to whom the baby boy has been born. If it happens at the synagogue, it will be immediately after the morning prayer service has taken place.

A trained professional called a **mohel** will perform the circumcision. The mohel will first of all place the baby boy on a special chair, which is called the Chair of Elijah. It is believed that each time there is a circumcision, the spirit of the great prophet Elijah is present.

The mohel then gives the child to the **sandek**, who will hold him in his lap while the operation is taking place. The sandek is normally one of the

A party to celebrate new birth

grandfathers of the baby or a person regarded by the husband and wife of especial importance.

The father will recite a special blessing for his son and the mohel will announce (in Hebrew) the name of the child. The parents will have agreed the name before the event.

The whole group present will also pray that the child will faithfully follow the laws of the **Torah** and be a good person. Wine is passed round and there is a party to celebrate the life of the new child.

The foreskin is taken away and placed in a small pot and buried as a mark of respect.

Most Jews will have their sons circumcised. When the Reform Movement first began, they questioned whether they should continue with the ceremony. They decided that it was an important marker for being a Jew that could not be discarded.

Jews also have a formal naming ceremony for their daughters. This takes place when the child is 30 days old.

Learning about religion

❶ Explain who the mohel and sandek are and why they are important to the circumcision ceremony.

❷ Why are Abraham and Elijah important in this ceremony?

❸ Using books, CD-ROMs and the Internet, find more about the ceremony to welcome Jewish girls into the world. Write down what you find.

Learning from religion

❶ Circumcision is about making promises. What promises do you think the parents should make to their child? Try to think of three and give reasons for your answers.

❷ Some people who are not religious feel that there should be a public naming ceremony. What do you think and why?

Becoming an adult

In this section you will:

- reflect on when a person is mature
- learn about the importance of the **Bar Mitzvah** and **Bat Mitzvah** ceremonies to Jewish people, their meaning and their symbolism.

When are you a grown up?

The French novelist Victor Hugo once wrote of two characters that 'one got older, the other matured'. When is a person an adult? Is that different from being mature?

In the laws of the UK, a person can be considered an adult at different ages. You can be held responsible for a crime at ten, be able to drive at seventeen and allowed to vote at eighteen. Why do you think different things are legalized at different ages?

Do boys mature more quickly than girls? Or is it the other way round?

Being an adult is when you are considered responsible. For Jews, Bar Mitzvah and Bat **Mitzvah** are times to mark the point when boys and girls become full members of the religion and when they can help to run the community.

Bar Mitzvah

Bar Mitzvah means 'son of the commandment' and marks the point at which a boy becomes a fully recognized member of the Jewish community. It is a time when he promises to try to follow all the **Torah's** laws.

A Bar Mitzvah at the Western Wall

The boy will practise wearing the **tallit** and will have learnt to put on the **tefillin** in preparation for the service.

The ceremony takes place on the **Shabbat** nearest to the boy's thirteenth birthday. For weeks before, the boy will have been learning Hebrew (if Hebrew is not his first language) and practising the piece of the Torah which he will read in the service. A **rabbi** will help him to do this.

The boy's father will pronounce a blessing on his son before he comes to read.

After he has read his portion, he is taken to a special meal to celebrate his Bar Mitzvah. Here he will give a **derasha**, a mini-sermon which allows him to give thanks to his parents and gives him the chance to re-affirm his faith in front of his family and friends.

He is now considered a full member of the **synagogue**. He can become part of the **minyan** and will be expected to keep the fast on **Yom Kippur** as well as other holy days.

Bat Mizvah

Reform Jews decided that girls should be treated equally to boys and so devised the Bat Mitzvah (which means 'daughter of the commandment'). It takes place when the girl is twelve. She too might read from the Torah and will promise to keep the law. She will also learn about how to keep the Shabbat and the festivals.

Bat Mitzvahs may be marked by a party to celebrate the girl's 'coming of age'.

Amongst the Orthodox Community, there is a ceremony called **Bat Chayil** for Jewish girls. This often takes place on a Sunday, rather than the Shabbat. They do not believe that it is appropriate for a woman to read a portion of the Torah so a passage from other parts of the **Tenakh** are used for example, from the historical books or the writings such as the Psalms.

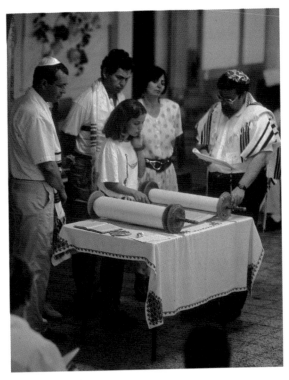

A Bat Mitzvah

Learning about religion

❶ Write a diary entry for a Bar Mitzvah boy on the day of his ceremony. Think about the preparation he has done and how the ceremony affects him.

❷ Why do you that these ceremonies are so important to Jewish people?

Learning from religion

❶ What is the difference between getting older and becoming mature?

❷ Do you think that Jews are right to say that boys and girls mature at different ages? Give reasons for your opinion.

❸ Devise a non-religious ceremony to mark a person becoming an adult.

Getting married

Why get married?

What sort of qualities do you think the person you would like to marry might have? Would they have to have a certain hair colour or like the things that you like?

Although a large number of people decide that they prefer to live with other people without getting married, many people still do have a marriage ceremony. Why? For some, it is because they want to make their commitment in front of God and their religious community. Others want to make a public and legal declaration of their love for each other.

Marriage is about commitment

The Jewish wedding ceremony

Most Jewish people will try to marry other Jews. This is because they will bring up their children in the faith and there is no conflict. Sometimes in the past, there were arranged marriages between Jewish families but these are quite unusual today. Some Jews might encourage a non-Jewish partner to convert to Judaism. They may ask them to promise that they will bring up their children in the Jewish faith.

The Jewish wedding ceremony usually, but not always, takes place in the **synagogue** and is called a **kiddushin**. The word 'kiddushin' means 'holy', because Jews think that marriage is holy.

Before the wedding begins, the bridegroom signs a document called a **Ketubah** in which he makes a number of promises to his wife-to-be. This is signed and witnessed by the groom, his father and other witnesses under a canopy called a **huppah**.

The bride processes slowly down the aisle of the synagogue and joins the groom, the best man and bridesmaids.

Two people will lead the service. The first is the **rabbi**, who will lead the formal and legally binding parts of the ceremony.

The **cantor** (a person employed to sing prayers in services in the synagogue) sings a welcome: 'Blessed be the one who comes in the name of the Lord.' He will also sing other blessings.

The bride and groom stand under the huppah facing the **Ark** where the **Torah** is kept. This is a symbol that they want their marriage to be one that follows the laws of God. The huppah itself stands for the new home that the couple will make together as a result of wedding. Across the huppah is often written a blessing for the bride and groom.

The cantor blesses a glass of wine and the bride and groom take a sip each. The groom then places a ring on the right-hand forefinger of his bride and says a blessing. The groom will also read the promises he has made in the Ketubah. The cantor will then recite seven blessings over the couple.

The bridegroom then takes the wineglass from which his wife and he took a sip, and wraps it in a cloth.

Placing it on the floor, he then stamps on the glass. This is a symbolic way of saying that marriages will always go through good times and bad times. It also is a reminder of the sad fact that the Jewish temple was destroyed by the Romans and has never yet been re-built.

The couple are now husband and wife. A wedding reception then takes place. No marriages are allowed on **Shabbat**, so Sundays and Tuesdays have become the two most popular days of the week for the ceremony to take place.

Learning about religion

❶ Write an e-mail about a Jewish wedding as if you were a Jewish child writing to a non-Jewish friend. Explain the important parts of the ceremony.

❷ Why do you think the Ketubah is so important to the wedding ceremony?

❸ 'You don't have to get married in a religious building to have a proper wedding.' What might a Jewish person say to this? What do you think.

Learning from religion

❶ In many wedding services, there are vows made between the bride and groom. What vows would you like your partner to make if you got married? Give reasons for your answer.

❷ 'Marriages are out dated.' Organize a class debate to discuss this issue.

The bridal party meet under the huppah

Death

In this section you will:

- learn about the Jewish attitude to death and grieving
- reflect upon your own ideas about what may or may not happen at death.

Ultimate statistic

The writer George Bernard Shaw said that death was the ultimate statistic, as one in one of us dies!

Whether we like it or not, it is something that we all face. How does religion help people face death and how can religions help us think about the important question as to whether this life is all there is?

A Jewish graveyard

Jewish funerals

If a Jew knows that they are going to die, then they are encouraged to recite the **Shema** prayer and ask God for forgiveness of their sins.

Orthodox Jews forbid the cremation of a dead body and insist on it being buried, though **Reform Jews** may allow cremation.

The body is washed and the eyes and mouth of the dead person are closed by a close relative of the deceased.

The funeral takes place, if possible, within twenty-four hours of the death. As soon as the family hears of the death of a loved one, they may make small tears in their clothes as a sign of grief.

In the past, there was great competition between Jewish people over how grand the funeral clothes worn by the corpse should be. Today, Jewish men are normally buried in the simple white clothes like those worn at **Yom Kippur**.

Jewish women are buried in a simple dress.

A man will have his **tallit** wrapped around him, with the tassles cut off the end, because he no longer needs to remember to follow all the commands of the law.

The body is covered by a shroud and then placed in a coffin. It is taken (in larger Jewish communities) to a **Bet Hayyin**, (House of Eternal Life), where a **rabbi** will lead people in prayers to give thanks for the life of the person.

The burial party carries the coffin towards the grave. They stop seven times to remember seven things mentioned in the book of Ecclesiastes. These include:

Working too hard
Believing that money will help you
The injustice in the world
A person denying themselves pleasure
Political power is fleeting
Relationships are fleeting
Death is a fact that we have to face.

As the body is lowered into the ground, the rabbi recites a prayer called **Kaddish**.

Grieving

Judaism encourages those who have lost a loved one to grieve.

For the first week the family sits **shiva**. The word 'shiva' means 'seven'. The close family members stay at home and others visit them. They offer comfort and pray with the family. Traditionally the mourners sit on low chairs during this week. This symbolizes that the whole body is 'brought low' by grief. Male mourners recite kaddish.

For the month after the funeral there is **sheloshin** which means 'thirty'. Male mourners visit the **synagogue** every day to recite the Kaddish. After this, things begin to return to normal, although some Jews will not go to parties for a year after the death of a close relative out of respect.

The third stage is **Yahrzeit** ('year-time'). On the first anniversary of the death, a Jewish family lights a candle. This remembers the verse from Proverbs 'a person's soul is the candle of the Lord'. They give thanks to God for the life of the one who has died. Close family members will hold Yahrzeit every year on the anniversary of the death of their loved ones.

Jews may have a gravestone with the person's name engraved on it. It is a tradition to place small stones on the grave at each visit. This probably comes from the time when Jews were buried in the desert and passing people would add stones to ensure the body was covered up.

Jews believe that if a person has led a good life, they will be rewarded by God. The wicked will be judged. The details of the afterlife are to be left to God rather than to be thought about now.

Learning about religion

❶ What symbolic things happen to the dead body before burial? Explain the most important aspects of what happens.

❷ Why do you think Jews have stages of grief? How helpful do you think these stages are?

❸ How might Jewish beliefs about the afterlife help them in the difficult moments of life?

Learning from religion

❶ Do you think funerals should be simple or grand affairs? Give reasons for your answer.

❷ What do you think happens after people die? Give reasons for your opinion.

God's world or ours?

A New Year for trees – Tu B'Shvat

One of the festivals which Jews celebrate is called Tu B'Shvat (a New Year for trees) and comes at the end of harvest. In Israel, they try to plant new trees as a sign of their willingness to help in giving something back to the land that God has given them, as well as taking away from it.

The Noachide laws

Jews believe that there are seven laws given to Noah which are binding on all people. If non-Jews keep them, they will be able to be accepted by God. The fourth of these laws is 'Do not be cruel to animals' (see page 50).

The Torah on animals

In other places too, the **Torah** encourages Jewish people to pay respect to other creatures and to help them.

'If you see your fellow's ass or his ox has fallen on the road, you must help him raise it.'

Deuteronomy 22: 4

A balance of nature

One **rabbi** once said that 'The world follows its own habit.' Jews believe that there are balances in nature which God put in place and that it is their responsibility to care for nature.

Planting trees is a sign of hope and thankfulness

Noah's Ark

'O Lord you preserve both man and beast.'

Psalm 36: 6

God alone is creator, but human beings are His stewards. They should look after things and they must not take unfair advantage of the world around them.

The rowing boat

Some people have used the picture of Noah and the ark as saying that being obedient to God will mean that you will want to show care for the environment around you, as Noah did when he obeyed God's call to rescue the animals. A group of Jewish scholars urged people to think about the environment in these terms:

'We have a responsibility to life, to defend it everywhere not only against our own sins but the sins of others. We are passengers together in this same fragile and glorious world.'

Learning about religion

❶ Why do you think one of the seven Noachide laws is about caring for animals?

❷ How should believing God is a creator alter the way Jews think about the environment?

❸ What does being a steward of God's creation mean?

Learning from religion

❶ Organize a debate that 'Human beings are a virus that has ruined the earth'.

❷ Should we have a regular tree planting ceremony?

Creation and the environment

In this section you will:

- learn about the meaning and importance of the Jewish idea of creation
- reflect on where human life comes from and its value to the world.

What a wonderful world

Have you ever stood at the top of a hill or looked into the sky and seen real beauty?

Perhaps you have watched the sunset go down on a summer's day. Or perhaps you have been struck by the power of a piece of music or a film has really moved you. Everyone can experience a sense of wonder, religious or not.

For the religious person, these experiences often make them think about what matters most. For the Jewish person, it may well make them reflect on the idea of God as a creator.

The Noachide laws

Jews believe that all people, both Jewish and non-Jewish should follow the laws that were given to Noah after the flood:

1. Do not worship idols.
2. Do not murder.
3. Do not steal.
4. Avoid sexual misconduct.
5. Do not be cruel to animals.
6. Avoid blasphemy.
7. Worship only one God.

Creation

The **Torah** teaches that God is the creator and that all that exists comes from God.

The story of creation in Genesis tells us that the world was created in six days and that God rested on the seventh day. For some Jews, the story is not so much how God created the world, but why.

At the end of each of the days of creation, the Torah says, 'God saw it was very good.' Jewish people believe that creation was made good and that human beings have a responsibility when it goes wrong. Humans have been given a special trust by God to care for the planet they are on.

'God blessed them (man and woman) and said to them, "Be fruitful and increase, fill the earth and subdue it, have dominion over the fish in the sea, the birds of the air and every living thing that moves on the earth."'

Genesis 1: 28

'The heavens tell out the glory of God, heaven's vault makes known his handiwork.'

Psalm 19: 1

| Day 1 | Day 2 | Day 3 | Day 4 | Day 5 | Day 6 | Day 7 |

The Genesis creation calendar

In the past, many Jews saw the idea of dominion, of ruling over the land, as being important because it showed the environment was purely for human beings to use as they saw fit.

Most Jews would now say that we are partners with the creator God and need to care for the environment around us.

There are ideas in the Torah that teach how to care for the environment. The **Shabbat** is a day of rest not just for human beings but also for the animals they use.

The Torah also teaches that the earth should be rested every seven years, so that it is refreshed.

In addition, the Torah says that, at time of war, the army should still think about the natural world around:

'When in your war against a city you have to besiege it for a long time in order to capture it, you must not destroy its trees, wielding the axe against them. You may eat them, but you must not cut them down.'

Deuteronomy 20: 19

Learning about religion

❶ Why do you think the Jewish faith has a creation story?

❷ Design a diagram to explain the different ways of understanding the creation story.

❸ Do you think Jewish ideas about creation might have lead to problems as well as protection for the environment?

Learning from religion

❶ Design a leaflet to explain some of the major environmental problems we face.

❷ Have you ever had a sense of wonder? Write a poem or design a poster to show what the experience was.

Moral issues

In this section you will:

● learn what Jews think about issues related to the moral issues of money, family and drugs, and how their beliefs affect their behaviour

● reflect on what you think about these issues.

Morality

Morality is all about choosing between right and wrong. Some people think that their conscience can tell them what do. Some, especially religious people, think that you need to turn to holy writings and find out what God would want you to do in different situations.

Money

Many Jews have in their homes small collection boxes called **pushkes**. They think it is important to give some money to charities, such as Jewish Care, which looks after the elderly and the disabled.

The Ten Commandments warn people against stealing or wanting things that are not theirs. In the book of Proverbs, it says:

'Do not wear yourself out to get rich; Be wise enough to desist.'

Proverbs 23: 4

In the book of Deuteronomy, there is an instruction to all Jews:

'Since there will never cease to be some in need on the earth, I therefore command you, "Open your hand to the poor and needy neighbour in your land"'

Deuteronomy 15: 11

The **Talmud** also tells of how being poor is a miserable fate and that people should be helped to escape its problems.

Family life

'Honour your father and your mother so that your days may be long in the land that the Lord is giving you.'

Exodus 20: 12

Jews believe that the family is an important part of society. This is where people learn to love one another and where children receive their first education. Jews believe that children should care for their parents when they become older.

Jews also see the family as an important place where the religion can be passed on, introducing children to the important festivals, the ideas of **kosher** and other parts of being a Jew. Some very strict Jewish families still arrange marriage partners for their children.

Family life is important to Jewish people

It is the responsibility of the parents to make sure that their children are brought up properly. The Talmud advises, 'Teach your son a trade or you teach him to become a robber.'

Marriage is seen as very important. It is within marriage that two people develop and become fully mature. Only in rare cases does a divorce take place.

Alcohol

Jews do not approve of heavy drinking, but they are allowed to drink occasionally. Wine is used during some religious ceremonies and it is acceptable to have a drink during some festivals, such as Purim. However, Jews discourage heavy drinking since it is improper to pray if one is 'unfit to stand before the King'. The Midrash teaches, 'Wine enters, sense goes out; wine enters, secrets come out.'

Jewish judges must not drink alcohol at all during their working day, and are not allowed to pass judgement if there is any trace of alcohol in their body.

Drugs can bring all kinds of problems

Drugs

Jews believe that drugs should only be used for medical reasons and have campaigned to stop drug taking.

Jews believe that as human beings were made in the image of God, they have a responsibility to care for their bodies.

Jews also believe that the illegal drug trade goes against the teaching in the Tenakh, as it will lead to the oppression of the poor. For example, in South America drug barons might force people to leave their land in order to cultivate drugs.

Learning about religion

❶ Write an article about a Jewish charity's work for a school magazine. You could write about the charities *Jewish Care*, *Norwood Child Care* or the *Chai Lifeline*. Use your library, CD-ROMs and the Internet to gather information.

❷ What problems might a Jewish teenager face given their beliefs about the family?

❸ Why do Jews think it wrong to use drugs for anything else than medical reasons?

Learning from religion

❶ What can you do to help people in need?

❷ Family life has changed in the last half-century. Does the Jewish teaching about family life still have meaning? Explain your answer.

Why is there suffering?

In this section you will:

● learn how the Jewish people have suffered from anti-Semitism (hatred of the Jews)

● reflect on how **scapegoating** can be a part of this.

Scapegoating

Why is it that some people are especially bullied or picked on while others are left alone? Perhaps they stand out in some way: they may have a different hair colour or a strong accent or a different colour skin. Perhaps they come from another country.

Sometimes, people have latched onto one group or another and singled them out for bad treatment. Perhaps they have used them to take out their own feelings of failure or weakness. This is sometimes called scapegoating, after a practice the Jewish people used to do when they lived in the desert. A priest would choose a goat and recite over the top of the animal the sins that the people felt were cutting them off from God. The goat would then be driven out into the desert to remove the bad things they had done. The modern scapegoat takes the anger or sense or failure of people today.

Jewish suffering before the Holocaust

In 70 CE, the Romans forcefully removed Jewish people from Israel and had destroyed the temple in Jerusalem, leaving only the Western Wall of its outer court standing. The Jews were dispersed around Europe, and this event became known as the **diaspora**. Without a homeland, many Jews felt vulnerable. When the Roman Empire became Christian, this often led to more problems down the centuries.

Jews have frequently been the victims of prejudice and discrimination. Christians often justified persecuting Jewish people because they had allowed Jesus to be crucified. Even though Jesus was Jewish, those who hated Jews chose to ignore this fact.

In 1066 CE there were Jews in England. Many were forced to become moneylenders because this was the one job they were often allowed to do. Christians were banned by the church from being money-lenders as they considered it wrong.

In the city of Lincoln, there is a house dating from 1170 CE which is called the Jew's house. It is made of stone, unlike the houses of the period (normally made of wood), so that it would not be burnt down.

In 1290 CE, King Edward I ordered Jews out of England and they were not allowed to return until the seventeenth century.

Across Europe, Jewish people were often attacked. In Russia, the ruler of the country, the Tsar, often picked on Jews, leading to more than one million Jews leaving the country in the 1880s CE. Non-Jewish Russians often helped the Tsar's army in the persecution of the Jews, driving them away from the places where they lived and sometimes destroying their houses and other possessions.

More than 100,000 Russian and Polish Jews escaped persecution by coming to England, while others went to the USA. In places such as London and Manchester, the new arrivals set up new businesses and schools.

Captain Dreyfus

In France, an army officer called Captain Dreyfus was wrongly accused of spying for Germany in the 1890s CE.

Perhaps the way to avoid persecution would be to return to the Middle East, many Jews began to think.

In the early part of the twentieth century, many Jews moved to the country of Palestine, to set up **kibbutzim** (communal farms). They built the city of Tel Aviv in land they bought from the local Arab population.

Kibbutzim still flourish today in Israel. Some have embraced not just agriculture but are also involved in factory work or specialist industries such as diamond polishing.

Captain Alfred Dreyfus

Dreyfus was a Jew and many believed that he had been selected to face trial more because of this than because of real guilt on his part. A young Swiss journalist called Theodore Hertzl was sent to cover the case.

When Dreyfus was sentenced to life imprisonment, Hertzl decided that as long as Jews lived in Europe, they would always be victims. What they needed to do was to return to the Middle East and re-start the nation of Israel. This idea was to become known as **Zionism**.

After a long campaign by many famous people, Dreyfus was released from wrongful imprisonment but it seemed to many that they needed to escape.

Learning about religion

❶ What is scapegoating? Why did Jews often suffer from it?

❷ Make a timeline showing Jewish suffering before World War II.

❸ Find out more about the trial of Captain Dreyfus and write your own play about the trial.

Learning from religion

❶ Find out what the following words mean: genocide, prejudice, discrimination and stereotypes. Then either:

   a write a paragraph explaining what you understand by each word

   or

   b produce a thought-provoking poster or display about one of the words, using examples from current news items.

❷ Why are some people more often bullied than others? Give reasons for your answers.

The Holocaust

The Holocaust

The word 'Holocaust' means a burnt offering. It refers to the suffering of the Jewish people in 1933–45 due to the Nazis in Europe. Their leader, Adolf Hitler, when he took power, began by banning Jews from parks, theatres and universities. The Nazis organized book burnings and, in 1938, they organized attacks against Jewish businesses. They also rounded up Jews and made them live only in particular areas of cities, called ghettoes. As World War II began, the Nazis set up **concentration camps**, with the intention to remove every Jew from Europe by systematically murdering them.

Escape from Sobibor

Most people in concentration camps had little chance of escape. On 14 October 1943, one camp made history as more than 300 Jews managed to escape from a camp called Sobibor.

A quarter of a million Jews had been murdered there. Every day, trains would arrive carrying thousands of people from across Nazi-occupied Europe. When they got off these trains, they were divided into two groups: the young men and women who had a skill were placed on one side, the older people and women with children on the other. These were taken to the gas chambers immediately. It took about 15–20 minutes for them to die.

A group of Jews found a way to organize an escape by stealing some weapons and then killing their guards. At the camp's roll call, their leaders encouraged them to escape.

Over 600 people rushed in the direction of the gates, taking on the remaining guards and desperately cutting through the barbed wire fences that held them in. Many were shot and some died when they stepped on the landmines planted outside. But over 300 managed to escape.

Some very religious Jews refused to escape, because they knew that any escape would involve them in breaking the commandment, 'You shall not kill'. Despite the evil that the Nazis were doing to them, they did not believe that it was right to fight back, if God had allowed them to go to the camp.

Following the escape, the Nazis closed the camp and covered it over. In the woods around Sobibor, there is a statue put up in honour of those who died in the camp, which had the words 'Never Again' carved into the stone.

God is hanging

In his book about his time in a concentration camp called *Night*, the author Elie Wiesel tells the following story:

'The SS hanged two Jewish men and a youth in front of the whole camp. The men died quickly, but the death throes of the youth lasted for half an hour.

"Where is God? Where is he?" someone asked behind me.

As the youth hung in torment in the noose after a long time, I heard a man call again, "Where is God now?"

And I heard a voice in myself, "Where is he? He is hanging there on the gallows."'

For some Jews, the concentration camps were so awful that they ceased to believe in a God of love. Others became religious, as they came to believe that there had to be something better than human beings.

The Chief **Rabbi**, Dr Jonathan Sacks, has written:

'We will never understand the Holocaust. But the asking of questions is itself a religious act. Future generations will ask: Why do we keep on being Jews? The answer is: to tell the story of our death sentence and our survival. And if they do not ask, we must make them ask.'

Learning about religion

❶ What different reactions to God did the Holocaust provoke in Jewish people? Is one reaction better than another in your opinion?

❷ Write a speech for someone who survived a camp like Sobibor to explain what life was like in the camp.

❸ What do you think Elie Wiesel means when he says that God was hanging on the gallows with the dying boy?

Learning from religion

❶ Does suffering make it harder or easier to believe in a God of love? Try to think of reasons for and against.

❷ Should war criminals always be punished? Organize a class debate on the subject.

Does God exist?

In this section you will:

● learn about more about Jewish ideas about God

● learn how the way they think about God affects the way they live

● reflect on what ideas about God reveal about human beings.

Does God exist?

'The fool says in his heart, "There is no God. Everyone is evil, every deed is bad, No one does any good!"'

Psalm 14: 1

A person who believes that there is no God is called an **atheist**. Someone who is not sure whether there is or is not a God is called an **agnostic**. A **theist** is a person who believes in a god. Jews have normally said that to be Jewish, you have to believe in God though there are some Jews who follow some of the religious laws without believing in God.

The question for most Jewish people is not whether God exists but what sort of being God is. There is a famous story that in one of the **concentration camps** some Jews put God on trial for ignoring their pain. This God, they decided, must be uncaring. They found God guilty of failing his people. At the end of the trial, they went off to worship the God they had found guilty.

In the story of Job, the character Job has to learn that God alone is in control. He says:

'The Lord gives and the Lord takes away; Blessed be the name of the Lord.'

Job 1: 21

God cannot be proved or disproved by an argument. God has to be experienced.

Job's faith was tested by God

What is God like?

Jews believe that God has always been there. God has no beginning or end: God has always existed.

Jews believe that God created all things that exist out of nothing. God goes on creating things, with human beings helping Him in this work.

The **Shema** prayer teaches that God is one. Jews believe that God is holy, that is God is not evil and does good.

God is ultimately in control.

God cannot be made into an idol. His name is too holy to be known. Many Jewish books use the expression G-D rather than God's full name. Jews must worship only this one true God.

God is Spirit and eternal. God alone is one who knows everything that will happen and has happened.

By the **covenant**, God has shown how He acts in history to make things better. By giving the law through Moses and sending His messengers, the **prophets**, God has shown care for the world and the chosen people.

God is the one true judge, punishing evil and rewarding those who live as God wants them to.

The universe: creation or accident?

Learning about religion

❶ Write down definitions of the following words: atheist, agnostic, theist. Which would you say you are? Explain why you think you are what you say you are.

❷ Draw a spider diagram to show the main beliefs Jews have about God. Do you think all the beliefs are as important as each other? Give reasons for your answer.

❸ Do you think it is possible to be a Jew without believing in God? Give reasons for your answer. (Remember that being a Jew is something that the religion believes you can either be born into or convert into.)

Learning from religion

❶ Select two Jewish beliefs about God and say how the world might be different if everyone shared this idea.

❷ In what ways does believing in God knowing what they are doing influence people?

Glossary

Agadah stories in the Talmud on moral values

Agnostic someone who is unsure whether or not there is a God

Amidah a prayer with eighteen blessings to God

Ark of the Covenant the cupboard where the Torah and other scrolls are stored in synagogues

Aron Hakodesh the focal point of the synagogue containing the Torah scrolls (also called the Ark)

Ashkenazim Jews whose ancestors came from Central and Eastern Europe

Atheist a person who does not believe in a god

Atonement being at one with God, normally by repentance or sacrifice

Bar Mitzvah marks a boy coming to maturity in religious terms

Bat Chayil marks a girl coming of age

Bat Mitzvah marks a girl coming to maturity in religious terms

Bet Din a court chaired by a rabbi

Bet ha Knesset synagogue; Jewish place of worship

Bet Hayyin the place where funerals are held

Bimah a raised platform in the synagogue where the Torah is read from

Brit Milah Hebrew for circumcision

Cantor person who sings important parts of services in the synagogues

Challah a plaited loaf used at the Shabbat meal

Cheder a school at a synagogue

Circumcision the removal of the boy's foreskin for religious purposes

Concentration camps camps organized by the Nazis in World War II for the extermination of the Jews and other groups they disapproved of

Covenant the promise made by God to care for the Jewish people

Derasha a sermon given by the Bar Mitzvah boy

Diaspora the forced dispersion of the Jews, following 70 CE

Exodus the mass flight from Egypt, led by Moses

Fast to give up food for a period to pray or worship instead of eating

Genocide mass murder of a race

Greggar rattle used when Haman's name is mentioned in the re-telling of the story of Esther at the festival of Purim

Halakhah the laws of the Talmud

Hanukiah eight-branched candlestick used at Hanukkah

Hanukkah an eight-day festival of lights

Havdalah the blessing ceremony at the end of Shabbat

Holocaust Jewish period of suffering under Hitler. Also known as the **Shoah** and the **Hurban**

Huppah the canopy under which the bride and groom stand during the marriage service

Idol a statue worshipped as a god

Judaism the religion of Jewish people

Kaddish prayer recited by mourners at a funeral

Kavanah the intention behind a prayer

Ketubah the marriage document

Ketuvim books in the Tenakh including Psalms, Proverbs and the book of Job

Kibbutz communal farm or village

Kiddush prayer of blessing said at the beginning of Shabbat

Kiddushin the Hebrew word for marriage

Kippah a head covering worn by Jews

Kosher food seen as pure and acceptable by Jews according to the Torah

Magen David Adom the Star of David

Manna bread provided for the Israelites by God when they had escaped from Egypt

Masada scene of mass-suicide of the Jewish Zealots in defiance against the Romans, now a place of pilgrimage

Menorah six-branched candlestick

Messiah 'the anointed one', a king that will be sent from God at the end of time

Mezuzah scroll containing the Shema

Midrash a collection of commentaries on the Tenakh

Mikveh Jewish ritual bath

Minyan ten adult Jews needed to make a synagogue

Miracle an act of God that suspends the law of nature

Mishnah Jewish religious books, the written down collection of rabbis' teachings

Mitzvot Jewish religious laws, good deeds or duties

Mohel person who performs the circumcision

Monotheism belief in only one God

Ner Tamid the eternal light found in the synagogue

Nevi'im the writings of the prophets and historical books in the Tenakh

Noachide Laws the seven laws that the Torah says all must follow, which were given to Noah after the flood

Oral law name given to the teachings that resulted from the interpretations of the laws in the Torah, subsequently written down in the Mishnah and the Talmud

Orthodox Jews Jews who follow all the laws of the Torah closely, and uphold Orthodoxy

Patriarch founding father of a faith

Pesach Hebrew for Passover, the festival that reminds Jews of how God rescued them from slavery in Egypt

Prophet messenger of God

Purim Jewish festival which reminds Jews of Queen Esther's rescue of the Jewish faith

Pushkes Jewish collection boxes

Rabbi ordained Jewish religious teacher and leader

Reform Jews Jews who felt that Judaism had to change the laws in order to update in line with society

Repent say sorry to God and trying to change the way you live

Rites of passage special ceremonies that mark an important event in life such as birth or marriage

Rosh Hashanah the Jewish New Year

Sandek the person who holds a baby at the circumcision

Scapegoating the practice of blaming a group for misfortune

Sephardim Jews whose ancestors came from Mediterranean countries, especially Spain, North Africa and the Middle East

Shabbat Jewish name for the holy day also known as the Sabbath

Shalom Hebrew word for peace and wholeness

Sheloshin thirty days of mourning after the death of a relative

Shema a prayer used by Jews affirming belief in one God

Shiva the first seven days after the death of a relative

Shofar rams' horn used in synagogue services

Siddur Jewish prayer book

Sidra part of the Torah read in the synagogue service on Shabbat

Sukkah small booths made at the times of Sukkot

Sukkot Jewish festival which takes place in the autumn

Synagogue Jewish place of worship

Tallit prayer shawl used by Jews, which includes 613 tassles to remind them of the laws in the Torah

Talmud Jewish religious book

Tefillin leather boxes used by Jews in prayer

Tenakh The Jewish name for the Old Testament, comprises the Torah, Nevi'im and Ketuvim

Theist a person who believes in the existence of a god

Torah Books of the Law, the first five books of the Tenakh

Vocation a calling by God

Warden a person in charge of the smooth running of the synagogue service

Yad a pointer used when reading the Torah Scrolls

Yahrzeit ceremony one year after the death of a loved one to re-call their passing

Yarmulka see **Kippah**

Yeshiva a college for rabbis and students of the Jewish scriptures

Yom Kippur the Day of Atonement

Zealots Jewish freedom fighters from the first century CE

Zionism the belief in the need for a Jewish homeland based in the Middle East, with Jerusalem as its capital

Index